THE VIEW FROM
THE SECOND CHARIOT

Dedication

I dedicate this book to the service of my Lord and savior Jesus Christ.

To my wife, Cynthia, of 30+ years, who encouraged me to write and supports me through ministry. To my children and grandchildren, Destini, (Rashad) Kierra Joi, Olivia, Makenzie, Rashad jr.

To my Mama, Christine Cherry, who has prayed for me and dedicated me to the Lord and has always been a witness for Jesus Christ.

In loving memory of my dad, Samuel L. Tucker
The Cherry family, so thankful I was born into this family
My Mother in love Mamie Blossom, who has been anticipating this project and encouraging me to go forward.

Acknowledgments

Thanks to:

Pastor Michael Spottsville, who led me to Christ and taught me the word.

Pastor Robert Griffin, who ordained me to minister.

Pastor Algia & Charis Blackwell & RCFC
who gave me a platform to minister.

Pastor Edward Smith, my prophet.

Special thank you to Bishop Darnell Leach and Overseer Dr. Anita Leach for praying for me and encouraging me that there are "no mistakes in God" and covering me.
Grace and peace NBF

Special Thank you to all of the choir members, praise team members, ushers, parking attendants, ministry of helps, armor bearers, adjutants, altar helpers, ministers in training, young deacons in training, and all administrative staff, the service could not run as smoothly and anointed without you!

And last but certainly not least, all of the husbands and wives and children of those who serve the second chariot who have had to watch you labor even in times you were not given the honor and respect, but the Lord sees and rewards you!

Blessings

Table of Contents

INTRODUCTION

I start this project quoting Pastor Ed Smith, who in a service one night, spoke these words, "You can get it done by grace." Those words have been a seed in my heart continuing to germinate even until now. I never intended to pursue any office in ministry, nor was I ever the type of person with the confidence to stand in front of others and speak or, God forbid, read out loud, but God afforded me grace.

So with trepidation, I embark on this journey called writing. I can't list all of those who I have allowed to speak into my life, because it has not only been human vessels, but God has used whatever He will, to teach and grow me up. I don't claim to have attained all that is to be known about ministry for I am still in the classroom of learning. One Pastor Robert Griffin encouraged me to keep a teachable spirit, and that I have done, not always willing but learning, not always encouraging but learning. Being teachable is not as easy as it may seem, see the student must possess the desire to grow in knowledge and be tested on the knowledge one has attained.

Proverbs 4:7 English Standard Version (ESV)

7 The beginning of wisdom is this: Get wisdom, and whatever you get, get insight.

I have learned that many misunderstandings that lead to hurts, pain and disappointments are due to the lack of the teacher themselves getting insight before they try to teach others. When I served in ministry as a young Deacon, I didn't understand what it meant to serve as deacon in the Lord's church and wasn't given insight into what were the requirements of the call to office, so blindly I stood and received the ordination and the certificate and smiled. Now what? What was a young twenty-four-year-old man who months recently was baptized into the body of Christ, had not had much or any church experience to go with this great responsibility. How was I to conduct myself daily when I went back to my day job? How was I supposed to dress on the weekend when I went out into the public? Was I expected to dress in the attire I had seen my elders with pressed shirts and slacks and an applejack hat?

You may have had good role models that were willing to take you into their tutorage and were good blueprints, and there were others you learned what not to do. You see a teachable spirit will glean knowledge and insight from good teachers and not so good teachers. But there is a sure word from Colossians 3:23 English Standard Version (ESV) [23] Whatever you do, work heartily, as for the Lord and not for men,

CHAPTER 1
When Dust gets In Your Eyes

As a kid, I grew up in a rural area on a farm and spent a lot of time outside during the spring and summer riding my bike and sometimes on the back of my papa's truck down dusty paths, and if you have ever had that experience, you know that the smallest grain of sand and clouds of dust can greatly obscure your view. And if the weather has been very dry for a while, you can expect dust clouds to rise and linger for quite some time. So, when following someone on a dusty road, if you don't know where you are going and the distance between you and the one who you are following continues to grow, you are in jeopardy of making wrong turns and even running off course.

So, when your view is clouded, you have to rely on your sense of hearing and follow the sound. The bible records in the book of Acts t hat suddenly there was the sound of a rushing and mighty wind that filled the whole house… It's vitally important to tune your inner frequency to the sound of the Holy Spirit, because when your view becomes cloudy, not if but when you will have to be on the same frequency as Holy Spirit and you can't simply follow the sound of the wind you have to be in a more intimate relationship. 2 Peter 1:21

English Standard Version (ESV) 21 For no prophecy was ever produced by the will of man, but men spoke from God as they were carried along by the Holy Spirit. *The gift of grace and humility is recognizing when you need to be carried by God, because the time will come when you won't have your moral compass or the confidence in your own instincts to give you clear directions. When your view from the Second chariot has been overcast by unmanaged emotions, and unclear directions Holy Spirit will help you navigate the terrain of unfamiliar territory. He will give His angels charge over you lest you dash your foot against a stone.*

Clouded spiritual view will cause you to make wrong turns that will lead you off course in life that can prove difficult to get back on the chartered course God had you on As free will moral agents God will not force your turnaround, it wasn't until Moses said, "I will now turn and see this great sight why the bush is not consumed", and when he exercised his will and made a furtive move then God called to him out of the burning bush. If you have ever stood beside burning brush or wood, you know the smoke will burn your eyes and cause you to be unable to enjoy the warmth from the fire that is burning, but you can still feel the warmth on your skin.

Following the leader is not as simple as it may sound, there has to be an inherit willingness in you to be led. God led the Hebrew children out of Egypt, but they only could see Moses as the one leading, yet it was the hand of God that actually led them. In a pillar of fire by night and a cloud by day, yet they still rebelled and murmured because there, hearts had not been conditioned to follow, due to time in bondage at the hand of their taskmaster Pharoah who drove them and forced them into whatever he wanted them to do. I heard it said, "you drive cattle, but you lead sheep." Some leaders come to lead by example, which may not have been a great example, and the model that was set before them was flawed!

Nevertheless, you have to recognize when you are being groomed to lead. There have been volumes of books and conferences held all over the world on leadership and have been extremely valuable and are the hallmark of the growing success of many Fortune 500 companies. These models all get their adaptation from the scriptures. Jesus Christ, the greatest leader that ever walked or will walk on the face of the earth, modeled leadership still transforming our world.

I offer this disclaimer, I am not a certified professional on leadership nor do I offer this writing as a guide to leadership in the 21 century, but I do offer tried and tested wisdom and over 20 plus years of serving in support roles and somewhat of an armor bearer, which I have seen to be greatly abused in some circles, more on that at a later time.

Jesus, the son of God, modeled the kind of leadership that is transcended in the way that those who followed closely could also create a following that was a healthy model that continued after He ascended to heaven. "Great leaders make themselves increasingly unnecessary." Which translates to me that if I model before you what the desire of the Father that has been passed on, to me you can carry out the task with minimal or no supervision. The task will be accomplished and the results will indicate that the instructions were followed and if any adversity arose, the spirit of the leader would know what to do if the master was not present.

CHAPTER 2
"Transfer of Spirit"

This term has intrigued me for years. (Numbers 11:16-17)
Numbers 11:16-17 The Message (MSG) 16-17 GOD said to Moses, "Gather together seventy men from among the leaders of Israel, men whom you know to be respected and responsible. Take them to the Tent of Meeting. I'll meet you there. I'll come down and speak with you. I'll take some of the Spirit that is on you and place it on them; they'll then be able to take some of the load of these people—you won't have to carry the whole thing alone.

Moses had received a great responsibility from the Lord, one that carried a great weight and required the wisdom of God to be tangible before the people. But the task was not meant to be shouldered by one man, it would require supernatural help that transcended above the natural wisdom of Moses. He needed help to shoulder the weeping of the people, he needed the kind of help that only comes by the grace of God. The kind of help that didn't have a separate agenda, the kind of help that would weave the same thread of God's justice among the people. Moses needed the kind of help that would display a united holy front before the people that the people couldn't pit the elder's wisdom against another to manipulate God's favor on their behalf. So God in His all-wise providence came down by His grace and endowed the seventy men with the same wisdom, anointing and ability to help Moses bear the burden of his leadership.

I will use the liberty to say that God transferred the same anointing that He had placed on Moses's life for leadership and placed it on the seventy elders. I use caution in saying this because of the abuse I have witnessed in the Lord's church in terms of those who serve under the leadership of others.

I do strongly believe that with humility as you serve in ministry or under the tutelage of an instructor you can take on the style of the leader that can be very effective in leadership and that the entire church or organization can move under one common goal to build a fortified structure that can stand during the greatest of adversity, scandal, loss of life or property and in reality the physical loss of the leader. I know those who know who they are in leadership and are not intimidated by those who possess gifting they don't have and I have also witnessed those who were not totally confident in the call on their lives and were intimidated by those who served under them.

Now granted there have and will always be those who only want to serve under others in an effort to undermine what God has established in a church or organization.

God hears all and knows all! He heard the weeping and complaining of the people and the toll it was taking on His servant Moses, Moses had received advice from His father-in-law Jethro in (Exodus 18), when advised Moses of shouldering all the burden of the people alone with all of their problems and complaints. Jethro seeing what Moses was taking on said to him, "this thing that you do is not good" (Ex. 18:17) NKJV. Sometimes our personal blind spots will not allow us to see the errors we are making even when trying to serve the Lord in all honesty.

The family dynamic of honor and respect in those days that Moses displayed with how he bowed in respect to the father of his wife and how he greeted him with a kiss of respect shows you need people in your life who can see those things you don't. Because of the "dust in your eyes" as you follow in the second chariot that may not be allowing you to be the effective leader God has assigned you to be. So, your family is a valuable resource that God has gifted you with. If God has gifted you with a husband or wife, father and mother, father-in-law or mother-in-law with the liberty to speak into your life, you are blessed!

I have learned that God often speaks in voices that sound just like your loved ones! We sometimes corner the voice of God as only able to speak in some dramatic way that gives us some physical manifestation as the only way we will accept His voice as confirmation. But when you become desperate to hear His voice when you need direction you will do well to not limit your hearing to what we deem as spiritual. We exclude God from our daily task because we view our lives only on two levels; spiritual and secular. However, God can't be contained to our ideology and our limited knowledge of how he chooses to speak to His children.

Psalm 139:8 Easy-to-Read Version (ERV) [8] If I go up to heaven, you will be there. If I go down to the place of death, you will be there.

For the believer, nothing is off-limits for God if He so chooses to use to speak to us and we are willing to tune our hearts. God often will speak through our leaders who have been before Him in prayer and consecration. We can also transfer the wisdom of God to others from those we have submitted to their leadership. Submit- accept or yield to a superior force or the authority or will of another person. The abuse and misuse of the word submit has caused great confusion and hurts that are difficult to recover from without the grace of God. In the next chapter, we will ride with one of the greatest to ride the second chariot, Joseph.

CHAPTER 3
"Riding The second chariot"

Genesis 41:42-43 Easy-to-Read Version (ERV) [42] Then Pharaoh gave his special ring to Joseph. The royal seal was on this ring. Pharaoh also gave Joseph a fine linen robe and put a gold chain around his neck. [43] Then he told Joseph to ride in his second chariot. Pharaoh's officials said, "Let him be the governor over the whole land of Egypt!"[a]

Joseph's onrush of honor came as the result of the gifting of God being recognized by Pharaoh who acknowledged that the Spirit of God was in Joseph. I hold to God's word out Proverbs 18:16 New International Version (NIV)[16] A gift opens the way and ushers the giver into the presence of the great.

God's gifting on your life will become evident without your manipulating the process, however discerning your "Now" season is developed as you are willing to serve without needing the spotlight to showcase what is evident in your life, and from your desire to please God. Joseph's motive was not to show how gifted he was, I believe his time in the prison was where his greatest development took place.

We give too much credit to Satanic attack of trying to hinder God's assignment for our lives when the reality is the issue of maturity. Now there is wisdom that comes with age but not necessarily maturity. Maturity and humility are the twins of development that should be at work in our lives no matter what capacity we serve in. My own personal challenge was I knew there was an anointing on my life for ministry but the inward conflict of resisting the arrogance also within. The most mature assessment of our lives is being honest about wanting to be seen as great in the eyes of people and falsely denying that we were just doing what God had "laid on our hearts." Knowing your authentic self takes some time to develop; it means realizing that you don't have all the answers and you have fears of being misunderstood, I believe the time Joseph was in the prison was the greatest time of inward development he experienced. One can only imagine how often his thoughts reflected back on how he got thrown into prison, the betrayal of his brothers' jealousy toward him and the lies that were believed about him. All these things were part of the process of development that would ultimately lend to fulfilling the assignment and purpose for his life.

Your view from the second chariot is not to prove you should have been at the helm from the beginning! It is a privilege to serve from the second chariot. It is not a demotion or a step down from who you are. It is when we think of being a helper and not the leader as a menial task. It proves the deception of arrogance that abides in our hearts.

Knowing who you are and who God has called you to be is the greatest and most rewarding inward peace one can know. We are admonished in scripture Romans 12:3 Easy-to-Read Version (ERV)

[3] God has given me a special gift, and that is why I have something to say to each one of you. Don't think that you are better than you really are. You must see yourself just as you are. Decide what you are by the faith God has given each of us.

For over twenty years I served as an associate Pastor. There were life lessons I have learned from the "second chariot" that has helped me to develop into the man I am today, learning to submit to God first is lesson number one, in doing so you come to understand that you will give an account to Jesus how you served. Were you part of the solution or were you part of the problem? If you can be trusted in the absence of the leader, you prove your faithfulness before God and not just render eye service. Luke 16:12 Easy-to-Read Version (ERV) [12] And if you cannot be trusted with the things that belong to someone else, you will not be given anything of your own.

Jesus stressed good stewardship in His parable of the unjust steward, a lot can be understood about ourselves in the area of how we handle money. Spending other people's money in reckless fashion proves you are not ready to assume the role of leader, whether in church or an organization that needs to operate from the standpoint of integrity at all times. I used to tell my daughters when you invest your own money in something, then you value it more.

Joseph proved to be a good steward, God's revelation to him in interpreting Pharaoh's dream also gave him the strategy to save the land and navigate Egypt through the adversity of the coming famine. The wisdom of God on Joseph's life proved he could be trusted and his word was as if Pharaoh was speaking. There was no dissention or separate agenda between the First chariot and Second chariot.

Riding the second chariot can be a ride on rough terrain and not always seeing the direction the first chariot is going. By this, I mean serving behind any leader will challenge your commitment to their vision, mainly because you were not there when the vision was given to the leader, so there has to be a "buy in" of sorts.

"Burn your ships"

I would like to take a sharp turn here, many years ago very early in ministry, I heard this phrase, "burn the ships," it comes from a historic conquest of history when in 1519, Spanish conquistador Hernando Cortez landed in Mexico on the shores of the Yucatan with the objective to seize the great treasure hoarded by the Aztecs, others before him had attempted and failed. Cortez was committed to his mission, but those who were with him had not been proven. It is said he was an excellent motivator and he convinced 500 soldiers and 100 sailors to set sail from Spain to Mexico and 11 ships to take the world's richest treasure. How could this small band of Spanish soldiers arrive in a strange country bring about an overthrow of a larger empire? It is said when they arrived, Cortez gathered the men on the shores for the final pep talk to get the final "buy in" of those who were with them. It was all or nothing. What he told them had to be the dumbest thing some were about here, and that was "burn the ships!" What? Cortez took away the option of failure to commit to the mission and also motivate the soldiers for the conquest. If they were going home, they were going home with the ships and treasures of the Aztecs who they came to plunder or die in the process. They succeeded. Why? They had no escape or just in case option. One of the many lessons in this history of Hernando Cortez is when you are second in line or third or fourth or fiftieth, there must be a level of commitment to the leader you believe you are called to undergird the mission to the conquest, but it will take you burning your ships for the cause. It does not mean you stop being who you are nor stop pursuing what God has called you to do personally. It means you are committed to the task at hand.

And I was not always willing to burn my ships! Riding the second chariot will reveal what true motives you are really pursuing. Are you willing to alter your course as you follow the leader? In my early days as a young minister, I served in ministry where I was one of 4 and we were given the opportunity to share the word on a given Sunday, and I recall having prepared the message all week through studying and fasting and prayer and Sunday service came, and the praise and worship went forth in the service and when I thought it was time to minister the word, the Pastor comes forth I thought to present me to the congregation to share only to say he believed the Lord was redirecting the service. He believed the Lord had ministered through praise and worship and sharing the word was postponed. I was very disappointed! And I tried to pretend I agreed but inwardly I didn't, so that festered in my heart and mind for days and that wasn't the last time that happened.

I learned that following a leader does not mean you agree with everything he/she does or says or even the leader was correct, that's for God to judge and not me. I, however, do offer counsel that in all things we have to follow the leading of the Spirit of God and honor

CHAPTER 4
The Dust of Jealousy

1 Samuel 18:6-9 New Life Version (NLV) [6] When David returned from killing the Philistine, the women came out of all the cities of Israel, singing and dancing, to meet King Saul, playing songs of joy on timbrels. [7] The women sang as they played, and said, "Saul has killed his thousands, and David his ten thousands." [8] Then Saul became very angry. This saying did not please him. He said, "They have given David honor for ten thousands, but for me only thousands. Now what more can he have but to be king?" [9] And Saul was jealous and did not trust David from that day on.

This scene of King Saul and David has played out among the ranks and files of leadership for centuries, and I know many Christ-loving fellowships have been the victims of this Satanic attack.

When riding the second chariot, this spirit will harass the unity of leadership until it inflicts its deception into the minds of unsuspecting servants and if not dealt with in humility and love, will divide and break up many fellowships, which has been the case for many years in the church and organizations around the world.

This luciferian spirit has perpetuated its cause from the ages when Lucifer was cast out of the presence of God and influencing 1/3 of the angels with him. This spirit seeks whom it may devour by using such tactics as "they don't know how valuable you are," or "you can teach and preach just as well as they can," or "you have always been overlooked," "I sing just as good if not better," Satanic influence is not an imaginary state of mind. According to Ephesians 6:12 New Life Version (NLV) [12] Our fight is not with people. It is against the leaders and the powers and the spirits of darkness in this world. It is against the demon world that works in the heavens.

Anyone who desires the office to serve in the body of Christ should be counted faithful to serve, but I believe the second most important thing is to gain insight into spiritual warfare! I had no understanding of the term as I served as a young deacon, but I became very aware as I became worship leader. What we fail to realize is that any office you serve in the church is a platform of INFLUENCE! If your platform of influence can be contaminated then you can become an agent for division and a stumbling block to the faith of others. Think for a moment if Satan influenced 1/3 of the angels in heaven whom God created, how much more will he seek to influence your platform and attack you in emotional imbalance or thinking of yourself more highly than you should think or even having a stubborn mentality that refuses correction. I believe one of the greatest lessons our Lord Jesus taught in the scriptures for us to follow has been missed too often for serving in any capacity of ministry and it is this John 14:30 Amplified Bible, Classic Edition (AMPC) [30] I will not talk with you much more, for the prince (evil genius, ruler) of the world is coming. And he has no claim on Me. [He has nothing in common with Me; there is nothing in Me that belongs to him, and he has no power over Me.]

Satanic influence seeks some commonality in us that he can attach to and use against us to doubt our faith in God's word, and cause us to be ineffective in the Kingdom of God. If there is any form of jealousy in your heart that has not been dealt with, it will be used against you and it will eventually be displayed in your attitude toward leadership. But what if you are like David whom the spirit of jealousy that had Saul bound is directed toward you, what do you do?

This can be a very disruptive and hurtful process to endure, like many of you reading have experienced. You will want to retreat in your effort to shield yourself or you may even try to suppress what God has put in your heart to make yourself unnoticeable so you won't have to deal with the jealousy, let me assure you it won't work! We must endeavor to keep Christ lifted up and not ourselves, you can't control how people will think or perceive you, so you have to keep your heart before God to allow humility to help you guard against the destructive spirit of PRIDE! I have found it was those times when God had used me in ministry that shortly after the spirit of pride came to collect.

I recall ministering at the altar and asking the Spirit of God to touch His people without the laying on of my hands and some fell under the power of God in the service, and the next day in our weekly men's fellowship prayer meeting the Pastor prayed for me I wouldn't become lifted up because of what God had done in the

service, I was offended, and reluctant to lay hands on people when praying for them at the altar again. This is what pride will do in your heart and in the fellowship of the saints. We want to be used by God to advance the Kingdom in the earth; however, there will be opposition that will be inward that is a continual process to spiritual maturity. David could have exalted himself and gave himself to the celebration of the women singing and dancing when he returned from killing the Philistine, but in his heart, he knew it was by the Lord that he got the victory and the honor he received was due to the Lord being gracious to him. Being used by God will cause jealousy against you and you will have to deal with inward pride but we have to hold to the scripture according to Proverbs 16:18 Easy-to-Read Version (ERV) 18 Pride is the first step toward destruction. Proud thoughts will lead you to defeat.

Pride, come down from there! Is the cry that must be heard in your soul, pride's destructive force can be so damaging to your life as you serve when you feel as though you have been overlooked and under-appreciated, the reason the destructive force has such great power against you is that it is not visible to the naked eye. It is a force that will stealthily grip you and pull you to dark places in your thought life and will cause you to compare yourself as being better than others and you long for opportunities to prove your gifts. There may be times you will have to wrestle with the spirit of pride with and audible voice. One way to recognize that you are being influenced by the spirit of pride is, you find it challenging to encourage others when they have done well, or you can immediately point out others mistakes by shielding it with constructive criticism. You will have to fight the good fight of faith against this subtle weapon, but you can win the battle. Self-deception creeps in when we don't keep honest accounts with God, and sometimes our drive for perfection is cloaked in the fear of being corrected when we error. No one has all the right answers and mistakes can be tools for learning.

Learning the flow of leadership will take time because leadership style will vary and once you learn the style of leadership in your church or group, you will have to adapt to promote unity in the spirit and the bond of peace.

CHAPTER 5

Chariots were not designed to be riden alone.

The history of chariots... Ancient History Encyclopedia Chariots were light vehicles usually built on two wheels drawn by 2 or 4 horses that consist of two persons standing a driver, also known as a charioteer and a warrior who fired at the enemy with a javelin or bow and arrow. The chariot was a supreme military weapon in Eurasia roughly from 1700 BCE to 500 BCE but was also used for hunting purposes and Olympic games, sporting contests and the Roman Circus Maximus.

The chariot was a moving platform from which soldiers could shoot at enemies using arrows and javelins by the fighter on board while the charioteer navigated the chariot. This is significant from the vantage point of serving as a couple in ministry. In some circles, the spouse of the one serving seems to not be considered as a vital part of the equation, but in reality, they are just as important to the success of the one who is called to serve. The two on the chariot will understand that both the warrior and the driver will have to focus when adversity strikes for them to have success against an attack.

Satanic influence is always in pursuit to attack the unity between those serving or fighting for a common cause, because unity is modeled after God's perfect divine order that is reflective in Genesis 1:26 English Standard Version (ESV). [26] Then God said, "Let us make man[a] in our image, after our likeness. And let them have dominion over the fish of the sea and over the birds of the heavens and over the livestock and over all the earth and over every creeping thing that creeps on the earth."

Division is not the character of God, He desires that His children dwell together in unity and love, when we endeavor to keep the unity of the Spirit in the bond of peace we demonstrate Christ to world, with one agenda and that is according to Deuteronomy 6:4 English Standard Version (ESV) [4] "Hear, O Israel: The LORD our God, the LORD *is one*.[a]

It is vitally important to endeavor to keep unity at the forefront in any partnership because that is where the greatest strength lies! If every church leadership team would keep this at the epicenter of their leaders, there would not be so many "spinoff" fellowships popping up on every corner.

The attack against unity is inevitable to married couples in ministry no matter who it may be. From personal experience, this can be some of the most intense warfare you can come up against in your marriage. A healthy church has Christ as the focus, and leaders who have their personal challenges constantly before God, and have come to the understanding those who desire the office of overseeing the lives of others here on earth, will stand before God and give account. And if we are to cause others to stumble in the faith and be scattered, this offends our God! Jeremiah 23:1-2 English Standard Version (ESV)

The Righteous Branch

23 "Woe to the shepherds who destroy and scatter the sheep of my pasture!" declares the LORD. 2 Therefore thus says the LORD, the God of Israel, concerning the shepherds who care for my people: "You have scattered my flock and have driven them away, and you have not attended to them. Behold, I will attend to you for your evil deeds, declares the LORD.

In Revelation, Jesus had specific messages for the seven churches, each message, as John was instructed to write was not generalization, but specific for the church that also transcended to the church age in which we live in. The Lord uses the phrase "I Know" which assured that He understood the plight of each church and the opposition and the persecution that each would have to endure, but He also gave observation of the works of the seven churches, which also lets us know that there is nothing that goes unnoticed by our Lord in our fellowships today.

We are called to support one another and esteem one another and we should hold our brothers and sisters in high regards because the unity of the church is what should be a part of the prerequisite of a healthy fellowship of believers. The same holds true in the marriage between a husband and his wife. Ephesians 5:25-28 The Message (MSG) [25-28] Husbands, go all out in your love for your wives, exactly as Christ did for the church—a love marked by giving, not getting. Christ's love makes the church whole. His words evoke her beauty. Everything he does and says is designed to bring the best out of her, dressing her in dazzling white silk, radiant with holiness. And that is how husbands ought to love their wives. They're really doing themselves a favor—since they're already "one" in marriage.

I am not against the order of leadership in the church or in the marriage relationship as modeled and commanded by Christ, period end of story! However, we must demonstrate the same blueprint that the bible presents. In the church age today, we interpret the scripture in ways that deify humanity and humanize divinity, which can be seen in some denominational fellowships. Again, I am not against denominations in the church, it is only when the denomination becomes the hierarchy above what Jesus Christ who died and rose again and established in the church. I am therefore no expert on this subject so I digress.

CHAPTER 6
Wounded Warrior

When the chariots were used in battle, inevitably, some would be wounded and become a casualty of war, which is why the charioteer had to be skilled and the one riding had to be sharp and avoid being killed as a moving target. I use this analogy regarding the wounds and injury that occur when you ride the second chariot in ministry. There are seasons when arrows are meant for the first chariot only to miss and land in the second. You may not be on the front line of a battle, but that doesn't exclude you from becoming wounded!

Some of the most hurtful experiences I have survived were those wounds I took for the leaders. When the leaders' reasons for a direction or new way of doing things were not understood by the congregants, there were times the arrows were directed at my chariot. I am a strong believer in that when one fights along beside you and will get in the trenches with you, then you should endeavor to protect your battle partners and not put them out there to kill. Now some will disagree with these sentiments, but if you are a leader and there is a change in the course that will be significant, then as the leader, you should be bold enough to give the new direction if it indeed came from God.

Many second charioteers have been wounded and became casualties because of leaders who did not consider this. 2 Samuel 11:14-15 The Message (MSG) 14-15 In the morning David wrote a letter to Joab and sent it with Uriah. In the letter he wrote, "Put Uriah in the front lines where the fighting is the fiercest. Then pull back and leave him exposed so that he's sure to be killed."

In this account in 2 Samuel 11, David is trying to cover up his weakness as a leader, betraying Uriah, one of his elite soldiers by exposing him to the forefront of the hottest battle. The word (exposed) stands out to me in this translation because it connotes being sent out to carry out a command with no protection from the possibility of being fatally wounded by the enemy. There is a measure of danger in the act of loyalty! Being loyal can obscure your judgment of making wise decisions that may get your character assassinated or your influence. Leaders should study the depth of character of those who serve along beside them to know their disposition in the face of adversity. David knew Uriah was a loyal soldier so he devised a plan to have him killed to cover his sin.

We can make decisions and accept assignments out of loyalty to men and ignore the Holy Spirit's leading for our own desires and willingness to serve. However, we have to be honest within to know where our limitations are at the current season in our lives. This is easier said than achieved.

The art of deciding has to become a learned skilled. I have been critiqued for being slow to make a choice and that's fine when times are warranted, but it can also be masked in a disposition of

procrastination, which is the greatest hindrance to moving forward. Being loyal is not a negative characteristic to possess; I believe it should be the conviction of a person willing to please God before men. Colossians 3:23 Amplified Bible (AMP) [23] Whatever you do [whatever your task may be], work from the soul [that is, put in your very best effort], as [something ***done***] for the Lord and not for men,

Consider this, many of us have been exposed to error for understanding the character of God by poor representation of those who have stood before us whom we have held in high regard; nevertheless, our view can become quite distorted because we have neglected to know God on a personal level. A denominational Jesus with a biblical view of Jesus has confused me also. I have also have been confused by legalism been touted for holiness.

Please forgive my memory on this one, but I heard it said, "Revelation of the word is not new truth, it's just truth finally understood." The Old Testament was the New Testament concealed and the New Testament is the Old Testament revealed. There are traditions passed down for generations in the church without biblical validation or contextual accuracy that has played a great part in the divisive and weakened foundations of some in the church.

Serving as an associate or assistant pastor is a subordinate position and should be understood that you can't take liberties just because you feel led to do so without the consent of the senior leadership. As an associate pastor, I served for 22 years before I transitioned as lead pastor. Sometimes, being the associate meant that I didn't have to dodge the arrows that the senior leadership would have to take. It also meant that I could not forget that even though I was serving under the leadership of a man, I was serving God through him.

Now, this can get out of balance if we don't understand what (Col.3:23) says that whatever you do, do with all your heart as to the Lord and not to men, which means being motivated by your love for God and people. This will get very challenging if you fail to ignore this principle. Love for God has to be our top priority in service, along with growing in maturity in relation to one another as humans in the church when relationships become strained due to offenses and feelings getting hurt when something was said in a tone that seems disrespectful.

Relationships in the body of Christ will always be a work in progress while here in our earthly bodies, and everyone will experience some hurt and disappointment in the church. The reason for this is the false narrative that we believe just because it's done in the name of the Lord that it is always from the Lord, that is why we must read the bible to understand the character of God. God is love, He doesn't come to a point of love, He just is.

There are strong, healthy church environments where the leaderships have grown to a place of maturity and realize that we are not only in covenant with God, but one another, where God's word has been preached and taught with understanding and discipleship is and ongoing trait of the ministry. Church pews or chairs are occupied by those who are saved but have had little in the way of being a disciple. What it means to grow in grace and walk a daily walk with the presence of God. Allow me to attempt to bring clarity, it has been taught that spiritual disciplines such as praying, reading the bible, and fasting are what makes us more holy, these are key factors to maintain spiritual growth and having a life of daily devotion is indeed necessary, but if we could discipline ourselves into holiness, we wouldn't need God's grace. His grace daily helps us to live out our faith, and I have kept these disciplines and felt like it was my accomplishments and all I seem to get were feelings of self-righteousness and missed the whole point of fasting and prayer. Prayer and fasting are ways we bring our flesh under the submission of our spirit that is now alive to God through redemption, we are instructed to grow in the grace and knowledge of our Lord and savior Jesus Christ. All growth is a process of development with adequate knowledge and understanding. Making knowledge applicable to your life in situations means you have come to understand what the bible teaches us. It doesn't mean you have figured out every problem, but it means you are growing in faith to the degree that your trust in God grows in your relationship with Him and there are no mistakes in Him or His word, and God is not separate from His word, for He and his word are divinely intertwined. He is not two-faced regarding saying one thing and mean something else.

Devotion to God should be in context as we serve one another and not to think of ourselves more highly than we ought to think, but be imitators of God as dear children. And walk in love, as Christ also has loved us, and given Himself for us, an offering and a sacrifice to God for a sweet-smelling aroma (Eph.5:1-2). When serving in help ministries, it will require sacrifice on your behalf and even your family's so it is important to understand that it is God whom we serve with our heart and mind, but I must acknowledge the abuse that can come because of human deification.

When the ones we are serving have been blinded to their own frailties of the flesh, what I mean is the lack of respect for one another in the body of Christ, when those who have been called along beside us to serve are being treated and talked to as if they don't possess their own minds to think.

I have very strong feelings when it comes to the belittling of another human being in the eye of onlookers or in the congregation of church members. In some church circles, the treatment of those who serve can't be distinguished from the workplace. And there are those who prey on the disposition of others who may not be as "strong-willed" in their demeanor as others. Most "strong-willed" personalities are morphed out of some personal insecurities and to feel good about themselves, they mask their insecurities by being dominant over others. I have witnessed some of my female colleagues in ministry who feel as though they have to project this oar of dominance to be respected in ministry, some are even applauded for their "no-nonsense" attitude when it comes to those who serve with them, and those who accept this treatment as serving the Lord. I disagree with this mindset that God can only bless me as it pertains to how subservient I am to another person. I believe Joseph understood that He was endowed by God and the vision God had given him and the purpose of his life was orchestrated by God. Even in all of his plight, the jealousy of his brothers, sold into slavery, the thought of him being dead by his father, the lies of Potiphar's wife, his imprisonment, and being forgotten by those he helped while in prison, were all for a greater plan that God had preserved his life for.

The real issue is about stewardship, how you manage what God has allowed us to possess. We are stewards of our call to serve in God's kingdom, whether it is with money or possessions or as it pertains to service in the church. If you have been called to assist the pastoral office, then you have been made a steward in that area and how you manage that calling in your life does determine whether you are trustworthy for promotion. If you are not the lead singer in the choir or the praise team, then you are a steward to lend your gifts and talent to the Lord through the leader that ultimately God's presence is what is manifested and that deliverance may come to the broken and those who need the salvation of Jesus Christ. Luke 16:12 And if you have not been faithful in what is another man's, who will give you what is your own? No matter what we must pass in the area of good stewardship, whether you are bishop, pastor, associate, assistant, choir director, praise leader, deacon, deaconess, etc. It is faithfulness the brings promotion.

The life of the second chariot

The life of the second chariot can be very fulfilling but also with built-in highs and lows, and overcoming feelings of being overlooked and rejected can seem impossible to get over, as I have stated previously I served for 22 years as and associate and there were times when I loved serving in that capacity and there were times I wanted to totally abandon my responsibilities and let the train wreck happen.

But I have to remember that in whatever capacity we serve in, it must be for the glory of God and not man. I believe our endeavor should be let's try to be a part of the solution and not the problem.

CHAPTER 7
How to manage your vantage point
Manage your vantage point 2

View from the second chariot

Genesis 41:43...he had him ride in the second chariot as his second in command. This life process of Joseph gives us the narrative that our vantage point from the second chariot can be one filled with great responsibility and opportunities that change the course of our lives and the ones we are chosen to lead as we navigate through terrains that are unfamiliar. Great leaders, I believe, are morphed out of adverse situations, which causes their God-given abilities to be displayed before those who need direction when tragedy or crisis happens. Joseph, who overcame some of the greatest challenges, didn't allow them to defeat him but they were the weights that built his faith muscles and developed his leadership skills and promoted him not due to his education, or ethnicity, nor even nepotism. He was promoted because he learned to manage his vantage point.

The bible is not just a good read it, helps us to get a closer look at the glory and awesome wonder of the one and true God who is and was and will be, it also gives us the redemptive plan He has for His creation, and it also was written for admonition and example with the creative power to renew our minds to see what God intended for the redeemed spirit of mankind. I believe we see with our minds; what I mean by this is most of what we see is a matter of perspective. There is the obvious of reality, what we see in the natural then there is the realm of the unseen. We all may see things from different perspectives,

[2] Do not be conformed to this world,[c] but be transformed by the renewal of your mind, that by testing you may discern what is the will of God, what is good and acceptable and perfect.[d]

There is much to glean from this verse, being born again should also be the new birth of a new way of thinking not following our former patterns of thinking before Christ. Our thought patterns are being developed from our youth, and the environment we grew up in have been the scaffold that supported these thought patterns we live our lives by today. Social and economic upbringing whether we want to admit it or not are major role-players. I used to believe in the tooth fairy leaving money under my pillow when I lost a tooth, but I grew up in a rural county and it didn't take long for me to reason that no such creature existed that came into our house without being heard or for that matter getting a serious beat down. But I was allowed for a season to foster that belief until the truth was revealed. What I am trying to convey is your perspective is shaped by the environment and truth you understand, so when it comes to managing your vantage points seeing from God's perspective is to accept His word into our lives as the instructional download that helps our faith mature into what was is really meant by (Phil. 4:13) I can do all things through Christ who gives me strength. Means that no matter my situation or circumstance, I am learning that whatever state I find myself in is that God is sovereign and He knows what is best. So, learning to manage my vantage point from what the bible teaches me as I live according to His precepts and statutes that are timeless. Even in our darkest times when we can't see the end of a trial or we are denying what is inevitable, that we know God is in total control and there are no mistakes in God as Bishop Darnell Leach often encouraged me with that exact statement. It really does matter how you see things in this world and know that a lot of what we see in ourselves and others comes from personal motives that need to be laundered through the cleansing blood of Jesus!

And know the world that we live in now is on borrowed time as we await the new heaven and new earth that God is creating through our Lord Jesus Christ.

[11] And the word of the LORD came to me, saying, "Jeremiah, what do you see?" And I said, "I see an almond[a] branch." [12] Then the LORD said to me, "You have seen well, for I am watching over my word to perform it."

God is testing the prophet Jeremiah on perspective and vantage point, what do you see? When you are riding the second chariot, you will do well to learn the skills of managing your vantage points and be willing to allow God to challenge you to change your position.

Luke 19 English Standard Version (ESV)

Jesus and Zacchaeus

[19] He entered Jericho and was passing through. [2] And behold, there was a man named Zacchaeus. He was a chief tax collector and was rich. [3] And he was seeking to see who Jesus was, but on account of the crowd he could not, because he was small in stature. [4] So he ran on ahead and climbed up into a sycamore tree to see him, for he was about to pass that way. [5] And when Jesus came to the place, he looked up and said to him, "Zacchaeus, hurry and come down, for I must stay at your house today." [6] So he hurried and came down and received him joyfully.

Zacchaeus had to change his position that changed his vantage point as Jesus was coming through, had he not been willing to do this, he would have missed out on visitation from the Lord. Sometimes we stay in places longer than we should have because we are not willing to give up our comfort or we have allowed the fear of the unknown to intimidate us from moving forward and sometimes God will allow trouble or as it seems fire to get us to move to the place of His purpose where He can be glorified through His church.

Good managers of vantage points are willing to be challenged periodically about their current view, because we all have those blind spots that need to be revealed.

CHAPTER 8
The Practicality of the Second Chariot

When we accept the call of serving, it means we are willing to do some things that may not get noticed on a weekly basis and it should because we have an inherent desire to see things operate like God, decent and orderly.

- *So, here are a few things I have learned;*
- *Just be willing to help*
- *Make your leader feel he/she can trust you to get the job done*
- *Remember the job you do has a reflection on you and your whole team*
- *Take the opportunity to become more skilled in what you are called to do.*
- *Be willing to get feedback on how you can better assist.*
- *Find out what your leader needs from you, don't assume.*
- *Clarity, clarity, clarity*
- *Ask for any updates before service if any*
- *Avoid public annoyance if something doesn't go as planned.*

- *Correct with grace and not bitterness*

- *Give your attention when instructions are being given out.*

- *If you can't be there, let the leader know as soon as possible.*

- *Work on taking things personal we are flawed creatures.*

- *Your personal devotion to God should never go neglected!*

- *Realize you need to be ministered so avoid overworking.*

- *Take periodic breaks to stay refreshed in ministry*

- *Avoid the temptation to publicly criticize those you assist*

- *Take your personal frustrations you have about those you assist to God!*

- *Confess your anger and frustrations to God!*

- *Never deify a human that alone belongs to Christ!*

- *Know that God sees all!*

- *Pray, pray, pray!*

- *If possible, live at peace. If not, don't fester. It will destroy unity and damage respect.*

CHAPTER 9
Pressing Through

Some time has passed since I last wrote, and since then, the world is in the midst of a global pandemic that has yet come to its fruition and a great challenge to the four-walled church structure, because of the crisis of COVID-19 and orders from disease control and governors, churches have been asked not to meet together in public settings. And before the next wave of disease was to hit, the world was captivated by the age-old pandemic of racism after the public murdering of an American citizen in Minneapolis Min. by the name of George Floyd by a white police officer. The sin of racism caused an outcry around the world that added to the already deteriorating fabric of moral ethics and decency towards human life. Now we a pandemic that is killing and affecting millions and the sin of racism that is on display and killing and affecting millions and the church is discouraged from meeting and physically congregating together, and my own vantage point has been challenged to its core! Yet my faith remains rooted in God's word and my belief in God has grown even stronger. The reality for me is the sovereignty of God has not only assured me that His word alone is true, but it has also revealed the false narrative from some that only touts a perfect health and wealth gospel.

The church has never been described by Jesus as a structure of brick and mortar, but on the revelation He is the Christ the son of the living God, who came to seek and to save them that are lost, and restore sight to the blind and healed the wounded and broken-hearted and set free them that sin has bruised. In many ways, we have not represented the Christ of the bible well to the world because we have tailored the message as if the gospel more about mankind than the God who created man. I praise God for allowing the revealing of the true heart and motives of man in the sight of the world. Currently, the race for a vaccine is on to combat a disease that hasn't been seen before to save lives and stop the spread of COVID-19, for some, it will be the ultimate victory to say we were first to market. The resilience of human beings is embedded in the DNA that God Himself created mankind with when He said, "lets us make man in Our image and likeness" (Gen.1:26).

Only the image was flawed due to rebellion and deceit from the wicked one who continues to deceive man into being deified of his own self and not acknowledge the God who created all things and sustains all things with the power of His word who is blessed forever (Amen). The sin of idolatry that results from rebellion is erected in our own hearts as it pertains to our image of a Jesus that is not consistent with the revelation of God Himself in the scriptures. We adapt our image of Jesus with the change in our current culture and mold him to appease our comfort, but very plainly, the bible says Jesus Christ the same yesterday and today and forevermore. This means that Christ is over culture! It means we can't parade Jesus through the streets arrayed in protest regalia with the latest movement slogans, and siding with a political party or any right-wing group. It is blasphemy to attach

Jesus to personal agendas not supported by scripture. Joshua 5:13-15 English Standard Version (ESV)

The Commander of the LORD's Army

[13] When Joshua was by Jericho, he lifted up his eyes and looked, and behold, a man was standing before him with his drawn sword in his hand. And Joshua went to him and said to him, "Are you for us, or for our adversaries?" [14] And he said, "No; but I am the commander of the army of the LORD. Now I have come." And Joshua fell on his face to the earth and worshiped[a] and said to him, "What does my lord say to his servant?" [15] And the commander of the LORD's army said to Joshua, "Take off your sandals from your feet, for the place where you are standing is holy." And Joshua did so.

Footnotes:

The truth I glean from this portion of scripture from the book of Joshua is that he had the courage to confront the Man with drawn sword because he knew God was with him, but at first glance, he didn't recognize who he was, we often at first glance don't recognize the sovereign hand of God in a situation so we revert to old tactics we used to somehow chalk up some victories of the past, yet not recognize the current state of the battle we face or the enemy we are confronting. A brother engaged me in a short conversation at work one day and said, "the devil is on my trail," and I jested with him and quoted Jesus, "get the behind him, Satan." But the Spirit of God quickly prompted me to say to him that it's not always the devil after you, but God trying to court your attention, the Spirit of God imparted discernment into my heart to let Him know that God loves him and has a better plan for his life than he is currently living, he said thank you, but I knew that didn't come from me. My point is just like Joshua, it may look like an enemy's intimidating pursuit and we want to know is it friend or foe and are you on my side or the opposing side.

Christians and non-believers will try and court God's favor and His allegiance for their cause when the reality is we should submit to His way of doing things and follow His commands and adapt to His leading. When the commander of the Lord's army didn't comply with what Joshua perceived he then realized this was no ordinary Man, but indeed a theophany of Christ, and to be worshiped in obedience.

Joshua's life, as well as Joseph, demonstrates how God transitions leadership from one to another, but the greatest attribute one needs to possess is willing to be the servant of the Lord. I used to be under the impression when I was young that to be called into any office of ministry, you had to have gone through some near-death experience or gone to a seminary school or even had some great testimony of an encounter with God like Moses or Samuel and Esther and virgin Mary to name a few, but God will have mercy upon whom He will. I remember what I know now all though I didn't know back then that the Spirit of God said not in an audible voice, in my heart that "it is not the dramatics of the one called but the willingness to serve me." Being willing to serve God is a classroom constant learning and passing test and failing miserably at assignments that God gives us. I have failed at being a witness when I should have stood for something I knew was contrary to the character of God. I have walked away from a pulpit and knew immediately I didn't communicate with conviction what

God said and felt so defeated for days, yet He counted me faithful and gave me other opportunities to witness for Him. None of us gets it all right in this life, yet we must resolve that God is faithful when we are faithless and be fully persuaded that it is God which worketh in you both to will and to do of His good pleasure (Phil.2:13) one of my all-time favorite verses. Which means sometimes I don't have the faith for the assignment, but He chose me, sometimes I have questions, but He chose me, sometimes I am fearful, but He chose me, for reasons I can't understand.

Joshua had a promise from God, he also had a picture from God from what he personally witness God do through the willing hand of Moses and imperfect ability to speak, I believe that Moses was challenged to go back and speak to the people who knew him before his transformation, that can be one of the greatest obstacles a convert can face. Having to go back to the very environment you once lived in and persuade men and women to come to Jesus. But when you have had a divine encounter with God through Jesus Christ and hear these words in your mind and heart whenever you are fearful or doubtful "Lo, I am with you even to the ends of the world" your confidence in God's word is ignited and your faith strengthens then you can speak and lead with boldness and receive the strategies for going forward and be well equipped to crossover your Jordan river.

CHAPTER 10
Can I Recover from this?

As I reflect my own path of ministry a lot of things I gleaned from observing patterns and trends. I first would observe the patterns and trends of others and the environment I was frequently apart of, learning the ebbs and flows can be a great teacher and give meaningful insight and a valuable resource to help others and develop strategy going forward. I believe in the importance of learning who you are and what causes you fears and peace and what is your threshold to managing stress.

Heart problems and high blood pressures fills the pulpits in many churches due to the levels of stress that are mismanaged. When tasked for an assignment and even elevated by God, there are arrows aimed at you and your family. Some arrows are obvious and some are aimed from enemies we didn't know we had and those, by the way, are the most damaging because they can come from sources, i.e., people who you thought were glad about what God was doing in your life. I will admit that it has been difficult to be cordial with people who you know really are not for you and your success is not on their list to promote.

I will confess that I have countered my opposition with passive-aggressiveness.

I am not proud of my faults and blind-spots, but the first steps to healing is to acknowledge them. For me sometimes that meant being passive-aggressive, but when you have been converted strengthen your brethren. I served from the second chariot for the better part of 22 years, of which I mostly enjoyed even though there were times I despised it, just being honest. Being thought of as you wanting to take someone else's place or you weren't the one who was supposed to be chosen for the position, can take its toll on you added that Satan is allowed to influence the situation. I recall I accepted the role of lead pastor of a church of which I am comfortable admitting it was out of loyalty not leading. Loyalty is a great attribute to possess and it is hard to find authentic loyalty in these days. However, I have always believed that if you were going to help someone do it out the goodness of your heart and greater your reward is in heaven, I just believed that!

Loyalty can sometimes influence you to do and accept things even when you feel that uneasiness in your stomach, you know you shouldn't, but because you want to be a part of something good, you accept, and if it is successful, you can lay claim to having a part in the success, life quote: be part of the solution and not the problem.

It took me 8 to 10 months to really admit that I had experienced burnout in ministry; some may not believe it's a real thing, but it is, and many experience it on different levels. You can burn out in the corporate sector and you can become burned out in serving, and many have experienced it in caregiving. My definition of burnout is when your desire to do what you once had fulfillment in doing has become burdensome to you and don't have the patience for it and you can't seem to breathe new life into it or cast a new vision.

One pitfall of serving is you can give so much of yourself and then fall into the deception that I don't need nothing in return and that's simply not true. To produce, there has to be fuel from within that generates a production, machinery has to have fuel to produce and so do people.

Many leaders fall prey to the hero complex, when we love being the one with the insight or knows what to do at any given time, we can sometimes long to be like the sons of Issachar who understood the times and knew what God's people were to do. It is not a bad thing to desire what God's direction is for the lives of those who He has given the responsibility of leading. We should all strive to know what God will have us to do, but in so doing we can deplete our strength.Jesus gave us the pattern, when the veil which was His flesh grew tired, he withdrew to a place and prayed, and it was there he was strengthened to carry out the Father's will. I was under the impression that you are to burn with so much passion for the Lord that you were to die empty.

I am not under the impression that the great Apostle Paul died empty; he just discerned that he had finished his course and his departure was at hand, he knew when enough was enough by the grace of God. Some may think this too weak of a soldier's mentality, but even strong soldiers know when it is time to retreat and rest and enhance their skills for the next battle, but with so little turnaround time for leaders in the church today before you finish with the sermon your mind is racing about what you will preach or sing the next worship service.

In today's culture, many pastors are bi-vocational in addition to managing their families and caring for the church's needs. I experienced this for a short time when I served as lead pastor while managing my daily family life, church responsibilities while working fulltime 40 to 50 hours a week, some nights leaving work straight to church to teach bible classes, I loved the responsibility and the rush it gave me and I had the blessing of a half-hour commute, that involved some great prayer time and fellowship in worship that gave me the opportunity to be as fresh as I could for the people. As time went on, the demand increased on my job, the demand on my marriage and the trials we walked through with our children and even the unexpected death of my father, who I also took on the task to eulogize and bury with the blessing of help from my family, and then a serious illness of legionnaires disease pneumonia that could have very easily taken my life, though God spared me with the help of a persistent Dr. by the name of Douglas Brewer and the wisdom of my wife and mother, I thought the more I ministered the more fuel I would gain, but that was not the case indeed God gave me grace for my assignment, but I didn't talk to anyone about the pressure I was feeling to balance it all. This will seem unconventional, but I had to burn out to understand that I was not depending on God for strength, I was depending on my stamina and my gifting and not His grace!

I wrestled for about 16 months with resigning. I had written a letter of resignation a year prior, and just when I thought I would submit it I would retract it and try to press until a fresh wind would blow. One great danger in leadership is allowing yourself to be pulled into someone else's crisis, I mean, we will experience some of the same problems as others, but the path to healing may not lead you on the same course as others. I thought if I could just fight through until the end of the year, a new year would bring about a change. It didn't happen. I was growing more and more depressed and discouraged. I complained to God that "I didn't ask for this."

So, now what? We try to "press our way through" (church vernacular), but the inevitable will happen, so you must choose humility and realize you don't possess the skills for that particular assignment because it was out of loyalty rather than leading. I had avoided a meeting with the overseer wanting to be sure that I was deciding and not my emotions or the emotions of others, but it was apparent that I had decided many months prior I just didn't have the courage to admit it. Once you can admit that a choice you made wasn't right for you, it is very liberating to a degree. Then the emotional highs and lows you experience of relief, sadness, regret, blaming others, anger, and being angry with yourself for.

You must seek some form of godly council with a counselor who you can be honest with, if you ask God He will direct you and it may not be someone you already know, because not only will you need the council, if you are married, they should be involved too, because the burnout will affect your spouse and children and it can conjure feelings difficult to process internally.

A resignation is the end of a partnership between two parties; some are amicable and some are hostile. I believed that my resignation was an amicable decision, but I harbored some hostile feelings deeper than I would admit. In Pete Scazerro's book "Emotianally Healthy Spirituality" which I strongly suggest and endorse, the concept of the iceberg was profound because only about 10% of the iceberg is seen at the surface, it's the other 90% where the problem is much deeper that you have to deal with. That statement is very true when it comes to how we suppress our emotions in the church and in general, in some Christian circles we are prideful when it comes to dealing with our damaged emotions and a lack of understanding when it comes to helping those who have been deeply wounded by their past. We often demonize what we don't understand then anoint with oil and with the laying on of hands we confess that we are healed, only to continue our struggles in private. The Church is filled with hurting saved people who will die and transition to heaven but live a defeated, joyless Christian life on earth, because we are sometimes ill-equipped to help beyond their deeper needs. We give the fish and the loaves, but we don't equip them to fish because when they launch out into the deep, they are pulled under and drown because their souls are anchored to an iceberg that holds them under until near-drowning til the grace of God gives them a push up for air and they surface for a season only to plunge beneath the surface of un-resolved emotional and spiritual pain only never healing from their past abuse, misunderstanding, harboring the fugitive of un- forgiveness of a parent for abandoning them, or divorce and infidelity and being discriminated against. These are only some of the 90% of the iceberg not allowed to melt by the wonderful grace of Jesus that says we can be free and we are free from a painful troubled past.

Even though Joseph was second in command only to Pharaoh and he led Egypt and the neighboring tribes through the famine, he still had an iceberg to deal with, having first being gifted by God to interpret the future, and the jealousy he had to endure from his brother's who sold him into slavery, and accused by Potiphar's wife and thrown into prison then forgotten by the butler and the baker. Having all these internal issues to deal with yet being graced by God to lead from the second chariot he did so with the promise that God had put in his heart was with him through all of the process, I say process because some might think these were mishaps, but I beg to differ, the sovereign hand of God was on Joseph's life the entire duration of all the things he endured for the ultimate purpose of his life to be revealed even preserve a lineage for the Messiah. So, if we can ever realize that whether you are the lead or you support the lead that every role is vitally important to preserve the heritage of the gospel of Jesus Christ for the next generation. Sadly, sometimes it's hard to see beyond our current view when riding in the second chariot, remember that we are but dust ourselves, and the dust of the ones we follow will get into your eyes and cloud our view. So, our personal growth in the Lord Jesus will lend to the clarity we need when times are challenging and we desire to quit and retract our support.

I do believe that times will come when you will have to go in another direction and follow the leading of God for your next phase of life and ministry, but if you know you are called to serve via the second chariot, then drop your anchor and serve God with gladness and flourish in the field where you have been instructed to sow seed and grow. People leave churches and ministries all the time, some for obvious good reasons and some for immature reasons; nevertheless, you will have to live with your decision. You raise your children to make good choices while they are under your care, and they may leave and go away, but if you continue to love them even if they don't return to live permanent, they still should know they have a home to come back to if things got too difficult.

CHAPTER 11
Chariots of Fire

2 Kings 2:10-14 English Standard Version (ESV) [10] And he said, "You have asked a hard thing; yet, if you see me as I am being taken from you, it shall be so for you, but if you do not see me, it shall not be so." [11] And as they still went on and talked, behold, chariots of fire and horses of fire separated the two of them. And Elijah went up by a whirlwind into heaven. [12] And Elisha saw it and he cried, "My father, my father! The chariots of Israel and its horsemen!" And he saw him no more. Then he took hold of his own clothes and tore them in two pieces. [13] And he took up the cloak of Elijah that had fallen from him and went back and stood on the bank of the Jordan. [14] Then he took the cloak of Elijah that had fallen from him and struck the water, saying, "Where is the LORD, the God of Elijah?" And when he had struck the water, the water was parted to the one side and to the other, and Elisha went over.

Elijah and Elisha represent the transfer of anointing from the mentor to his mentee; I believe it is a valuable resource to have someone who is willing and called by God to mentor you. According to tradition, a man's principle heir was to receive a double portion of his material goods. However, Elisha didn't ask for wealth; he witnessed that the empowerment of God was and is greater than any wealth. The chariots of fire represent there is from heaven the endorsement of transferring power between two parties.

As before mentioned Moses to Joshua and Jewish tradition before the father died, he would call the sons to the bedside and bless them, I have also witnessed this, about a week before my wife's grandmother passed away we went to see her, she was suffering from slight dementia, but she recognized her children and grandchildren, so my wife went and set on the bed with her and she put both hands on my wife's face and told her how pretty she was then she said these words to her, "take all that stuff and ball it up and throw it in the trash" she had not shared anything prior to our visit but what I believe was God speaking to my wife from heaven where her grandmother was about to transition and give her instructions that heal her heart from past pain and a principle to live by going forward, it was a solemn moment.

But I shared that to say when you serve faithfully under the call of another who has the heart of God and the value of faithful service qualifies you to receive a greater empowerment of God's Spirit on your life, not everyone can have that experience. It was evident when God magnified Joshua in the eyes of the people when Moses died and when Elijah was taken up in a whirlwind at the appearance of the chariots of fire and at the ascension of Jesus after His resurrection and on the day of Pentecost when God poured out the Holy Spirit.

The ultimate goal is the empowerment of Holy Ghost poured out on His people to be the witnesses for the preservation and caring out the gospel Jesus Christ to the world. It's not about how well you can sing or teach or preach, but the act of submission and humility and to be faithful in that which is someone else's. The level of immaturity at which has been displayed in the church is not the will of God. I have been in this position myself. The truth is in these last days of what is being called the "new normal," we have to regain the structure and order in God's house and the credibility to be the light in a world being filled with gross darkness due to the lack of honor and respect for God's kingdom.

Amos 4:10 "I sent among you a plague after the manner of Egypt; your young men I killed with a sword, along with captive horses; I made a stench of your camps come up in your nostrils; Yet you have not returned to Me Says the Lord.

We can glean truth from the prophet Amos what happens when God's people won't accept correction, God in His mercy allows plagues and destructions to get our attention, yet we still jockey for positions in ministries and churches so can look the part having a form of godliness but denying the power. I pray before the publishing of this writing that the church would lead the world in repentance and not defiance. And instead of asking for the wealth of the sinner that is laid up for the just what are the motives for it anyway?

If your view from the second chariot is only about your personal gain and notoriety and not the preservation of testimony of Christ, then your view is clouded and your vantage point is obscured. Learn to serve the Lord with gladness even when the one you follow has drifted off the course God has planted you there for the stability of others who may not have come to maturity. Let your desire to serve be that of esteeming others.

Confrontation is necessary and can be done in a mature respectful way; avoiding confrontation will not bring resolution and can painful and discouraging when you feel that nothing was accomplished. I have had to have some difficult confrontations which were the beginning of the end of a partnership even though we all left saying we were glad we had the meeting, when all it really did was reveal how we felt in the first place only now it wasn't a secret, and the days or weeks after it turned even more "salty."

Sometimes, by the time you have had a meeting, the damage is already beyond repair and you are just going through the motions, but if you are skilled in counseling, you can put out some blazing fires of emotions with affirming statements such as, "I understand how that made you feel" "I was wrong for my tone with you."

Having the liberty to express how you feel without becoming adversarial should always be the goal in confrontation. Public confrontations should be a last resort unless it is severely jeopardizing the peace and safety of others some things are better left unaddressed unless there are dangerous patterns developing.

Controlling people will sometimes play victim when confronted about their behavior. It may be ideal to take notes during a confrontation to clarify what may have transpired for later reflection. Never confront when you are very, very angry; you may not be able to reel in your emotions fast enough and things get way out of hand.

I felt the need to share these tips because I have had these experiences as many of you have. There is a time and season for everything under the sun. (Eccl. 3) We must at all times keep loving our brother and sister at the forefront of any confrontation, and if all possible life at peace with all men.

Having served in a second chariot capacity for over twenty years have taught me many valuable lessons, some I am just coming to grasp, when you are not the senior leadership in a church or any organization, you are subject to said leader and even though you may feel that your perspective is better, it doesn't mean you have the liberty to enact it without leadership approval. I have also learned that personalities very seldom change and how you allow someone else's personality to affect you is entirely subject to you. One conviction I live by is not to let any human being's personality dictate the way I respond to God or if my spirit is always unrest when I'm around and individual or group. God alone is who I worship in honor and adoration, it doesn't mean I don't respect a person for the call on their life or the office they serve. We should hold one another in the highest esteem in the fear and admonition of the Lord in whose image we are created. Let God's love prevail in every situation and be subject to leading of the Holy Ghost and keep a teachable spirit and God who sits in heaven will promote you.

Joseph's view from the second chariot was like a behind the scenes assignment all about God's purpose flowing through the life of an individual who experienced God's providence in the life of a human. There is no public success without dedicated people who are committed behind the scenes who understand what is their purpose and calling in life. Man does not make it to the moon without the people on the ground, delicious food doesn't come to your table in a restaurant unless a great chef is behind the scenes in the kitchen and reconciliation of mankind wasn't possible unless God was in Christ reconciling man to himself.

We follow God's blueprint when we work from the second chariot, God was the orchestrator in all the Joseph was able to accomplish from the second chariot so that His good and perfect will would be done. Even if you are not the lead or the director and it seems that your dedication is going unnoticed and unappreciated remember even though the butler forgot Joseph, God didn't! (Hebrews 6:10) For God is not unjust to forget your work and labor of love which you have shown toward His name, in that you have ministered to the saints, and do minister (Heb.6:10). God never forgets any act of love and service done with righteous motives in His name. Many have become great leaders because they passed the test of faithfulness working from the second chariot. Maybe you are being groomed for the leadership in the first chariot, but the second chariot may be your kingdom assignment by God. So, how do you know if that is my assignment? One way to recognize is do you sense the anointing of God as you serve the second chariot? And does your gift flow with freedom and it is not laborious? In many services as I served as an associate pastor, my job was to ensure the sound equipment operated with perfection and that the pastor or minister didn't have to call for adjustments while speaking. I also would arrive before the start of service for sound checks, and to prepare the atmosphere for worship, something we often take for granted, we should long for a time in the presence of God as it was when the temple was dedicated to the Lord and God's presence was manifested in such a way that the priest could not stand to minister because He was pleased with the work of the temple and the motives to which it was built. (ref. 2 Chron. 7) As you serve in a second chariot role you are fulfilling acts of humility and God sees it as worship.

My journey in the second chariot has been rewarding and filled with turns and battles, but God has always sustained me and taught me and revealed Himself to me in ways I never imagined. Many who serve week after week and year after year as choir members, praise and worship teams, ushers, pastors aids, parking attendants, nursery helpers, church custodians, deacons, deaconess, church staff, and administrative assistants, your dedication and commitment make you an essential part of the worship of our Lord Jesus Christ. Your service like Joseph's is used by God for His good and perfect will so the gospel of Christ Jesus can flow and reach souls and convert hearts to Jesus. Serve the Lord with gladness!

CHAPTER 12
Finally
The passing of the reigns

Pharaoh's decision to pass the reigns to Joseph seems to be an unconventional move, but the reality was he came to realize that the wisdom that was in Joseph was beyond the knowledge of the Egyptian gods, and he also realized that if the nation was going to survive the demise of a severe famine he would have to entrust all of his wealth and resources into the hands of another who was not born in his house. Despite being perceived as a weak leader in the eyes of the nation and others, he proved to have enough foresight that not only would they survive the famine but would prosper in a greater way. By transferring such leadership and authority to another proved his leadership and he was comfortable enough to look like a fool in the eyes of many yet proving that his leadership had progressed to the level of oversight and confidence that someone else can carry the torch to the next level. I have heard the saying that "everything rises and falls on leadership," I believe there is a lot of truth to this statement; that's why you must choose with wisdom those you have the responsibility to mentor and promote. Leading behind leaders is part of growth and development of one's character. Every strong and enduring structure begins with scaffolding this exoskeleton is designed to support the outer construction until the building is fortified enough to stand on its on foundation, without a solid and committed supporting cast nothing can truly be called successful, it takes various levels of talent, skill set, and strength to become a compilation not a contest yet with someone who has vision and knows where the team needs to go and is able to navigate during adversity while grooming a successor.

So, how do you know when it's time to even begin the thought process of identifying a successor? This is a broad question to answer; my thoughts are all I can offer at this juncture. The first thought would concern the age of the leadership, but that's not always the case. I recall my first pastor who led me to Christ announced that the Lord was leading him to become a part of Promise Keepers ministry, I actually felt devastated at first because I had just recently gotten saved and he was a great inspiration and I wanted to learn under his tenure as pastor and being young in the faith, I thought that I wouldn't survive as a new Christian without him. But now I realized that you have to fulfill the calling God has on your life and be willing to follow His leading. His decision to follow his passion for ministry and transfer leadership to another still inspires me today. When the Spirit of God gave Apostle Paul the ministry of establishing churches, He also gave him the liberty to place pastors and elders over these fellowships and then he would go on to his next assignment. I am sure these elders felt as I did at first when Paul would leave, but Paul knew what his commission was from the Lord and it proved he was doing the will of God. I use this analogy to say everyone has their assignment from the Lord and it does not mean where you start is your final place of kingdom service.

Second, knowing when it's time to pass the reins of leadership, you have to know that you have prepared the successor and that God has chosen them and not you. Out of all of Jesse's sons, David was not the likely candidate to be chosen as king, because God chose Him, he only used the prophet to identify him. You must allow God to identify your successor, it could well be in your own house or one God has raised up. Jonathan, the son of Saul was heir in accordance to kingdom monarchy, but God chose David instead and Jonathan knew it and accepted that David was to be king instead of him. Sometimes nepotism can cloud our judgment when it comes to passing the reins of leadership and it is why prayer and fasting are necessary for getting clear direction from the Holy Spirit of God. Some selections today still resemble the casting of lots as it was in the old covenant. I do believe a church fellowship comprised of Spirit-filled council can seek the Lord and identify a successor if the absence occurs or death of a leader. This can be a difficult process with no previous guidelines in place or if there are family dynamics involved and if the board of directors does not have a proper balance whereas if voting is enacted that the majority vote will be weighted by close relatives who serve as directors.

As a certified church consultant, I strongly believe that a board of directors should be as diverse as possible for the sake of integrity for the ministry and accountability.

Also, when applying for 501c3 status, it is advised not to have an overrepresentation of family members on the board of directors and it should be on rotational terms for members serving on a board. A strong board of directors should resemble when Aaron and Hur held up Moses's hands, they will be there to help you make decisions in tough times and lead well in good times. Your ability to succeed will depend on those who surround you.

Joseph was chosen by God, but he was appointed by Pharaoh to the second chariot, it wasn't political advancement that Joseph sought after nor was it personal gain he had been prepared and chosen with a greater purpose in the mind of God to "preserve much people alive." I believe that God's plan is always looking beyond our current season and He chooses whom He promotes. Many have served in ministry behind great leaders and thought that transferring leadership would fall to them and many situations that has been the case, but many have felt rejected and when they were not chosen to succeed the outgoing leader. We must come to maturity that God knows best and come to the place that honor is not predicated on your ability to lead, but your willingness to serve God in whatever capacity He chooses. Remember, the front lines take on much of the assault in conflict, but a strong second line of defense helps creates the fortitude that enables the army to avoid being ambushed.

Works Cited

"Access Your Bible from Anywhere." BibleGateway.com: *A Searchable Online Bible in over 150 Versions and 50 Languages.*, www.biblegateway.com/.

Bagnall, Roger S. *The Encyclopedia of Ancient History.* Wiley-Blackwell, 2013.

Bagnall, Roger S. *The Encyclopedia of Ancient History.* Wiley-Blackwell, 2013.

"Emotionally Healthy Spirituality: Unleash a Revolution in Y our Life In Christ by Peter Scazzero." *Goodreads,* Goodreads, 29 June 2006, www.goodreads.com/book/show/249014.Emotionally_Healthy_Spirituality.

"Main Page." Wikipedia, Wikimedia Foundation, 10 Nov. 2020, en.wikipedia.org/wiki/Main_Page.